# WORLD'S CUTEST
# BABY ANIMALS
## in 3-D

# CONTENTS

Nature has given us mighty hunters, graceful athletes, and majestic giants that roam the land and oceans. But even the biggest and fiercest of these creatures starts out as a newborn, and so many of them are simply adorable. Find out more about these fluffy friends as you coo over their cuteness!

# BEAR CUBS

Bears come in all sorts of sizes, from the small sun bear to enormous brown bears and polar bears. But all eight species start life as tiny cubs, no bigger than a rabbit. In fact, bears have the tiniest babies (compared to their full grown size) of any mammal. The teeny cubs drink their mother's rich milk for at least a year to put on weight as fast as possible.

## BROWN BEARS

The famous grizzly bear is a type of brown bear. The cubs are born in winter while their mother is hibernating. They are tiny when they creep out of their den in the spring but soon grow big enough to wrestle and climb. The mother will push them up a tree with her nose to help them get the hang of it.

## AMERICAN BLACK BEAR

Like all bear cubs, black bears are blind, toothless, and helpless when they are born. Their eyes open after about a month, and they begin to walk about a week later. A bear mother will often carry her cub in her mouth to rescue it from danger.

## COASTAL BROWN BEAR

Brown bears that live on the coasts of Alaska and Russia grow much bigger than mountain brown bears. The cubs stay with their mother for up to two years, learning how to look after themselves. They have an excellent sense of smell for finding food, and eat just about anything!

## GIANT PANDA

Panda cubs are even smaller than other bear cubs. They are bald and pink, only about the size of a bar of soap. Their black and white markings appear when they are around a month old.

## POLAR BEARS

A pregnant polar bear digs a den in a snowdrift, so her babies are born out of harm's way. They learn to walk when they are about two months old, and eventually follow their mother above ground to start to feed on seal blubber. Hunting for seals is a tricky business, and cubs don't usually manage until they're over a year old. Polar bears are excellent swimmers, and the cubs enter the water when they are very young.

# DID YOU KNOW?

A polar bear's feet are webbed to help it swim and walk on snow. The bottom of its paws are furry to keep them warm.

# BIG KITTENS

Tigers, lions, leopards, and sometimes cheetahs are often grouped together as big cats. If you look at the adults, it's easy to see why. They are large, muscular, heavy creatures, built for hunting. However, even big cats start out small and cute! The mothers and babies communicate by purring, which is like a whisper to avoid being heard by their enemies.

## LEOPARD CUB
Grown leopards spend a lot of their time up trees, so the cubs need to learn how to climb. A spot high in the branches keeps them safe while they sleep and eat.

## CHEETAH CUB
Cheetah cubs are much fluffier than their parents. They have a mantle of long, tall hair down their back. This may help to camouflage them in long grass. A cheetah usually has two to four babies at one time, and looks after them until they are two years old.

## TIGER CUB
Big cat cubs love to play. They wrestle and chase and pounce in preparation for hunting when they grow up. However, they love to sleep, too! Adult tigers spend up to twenty hours each day snoozing or just lying in the shade.

## GETTING AROUND
Like most wild cats, a tiger mother will keep her cubs hidden for the first few months. She will move them around from den to den to prevent other killers from sniffing them out.

## LION CUBS

Lions live in large family groups, called prides, but a lioness will go off on her own when she is ready to give birth. She finds somewhere that is covered with plants to hide in while her cubs are tiny. They are born with their eyes closed, and start to see after about a week. A month or two later, they return to the pride, where many different females will feed them milk, not just their own mother.

## DID YOU KNOW?

Lion cubs have patterned fur when they are young, but the spots or rosettes disappear as they get older.

# ELEPHANTS

Adult elephants are the largest animals on land, so their babies are bigger than most, too! They still look small compared to their parents, and are lively, nosy, clumsy, and just adorable. They measure around 3.5 feet (1 m) tall at birth, which is the height of an average 4-year-old boy, and grow quickly in their first ten years.

## AFRICAN ELEPHANT

Elephants live on two continents: Africa and Asia. The African species have larger ears when they are fully grown. Both species have "fingers" on the end of their trunk. African elephants have two fingers so they can hold objects, but Asian elephants have just one finger and wrap their trunk around things to grab them.

## FURRY BABIES

Although it is wrinkled from the start, an elephant's skin changes as it grows. Very young calves are covered in fluffy red or black hair, which is replaced by soft bristles when they are older.

## PATIENT PARENT

Elephants are pregnant for almost 22 months – nearly two years! That's the longest that any mammal carries its baby before giving birth.

## FEEDING TIME

An elephant's trunk is its nose, not its mouth, so the baby has to snuggle right under its mother to drink her milk with its mouth. As they grow older, elephants drink less milk, and eat more adult food: grass, twigs, leaves, tree bark, and fruit. A grown elephant eats around 330 pounds (150 kg) of food every day – about the weight of two adult humans!

## DID YOU KNOW?

Baby elephant trunks are short. As they grow, the elephant has to get used to it, and quite often trips over its own trunk!

# GIRAFFES AND ZEBRAS

These hoofed creatures are common in Africa, and have very distinctive coat patterns. Both of them live in herds and roam great distances looking for food. They are fast runners, too – much faster than a top human sprinter!

## CHANGING STRIPES
A baby zebra has brown and white stripes, which change gradually as it gets older. The black and white stripes of an adult are different on every single animal, like a human fingerprint.

## RUDE AWAKENING
A female giraffe gives birth standing up. The newborn baby (called a calf) drops 5 feet (1.5 m) to the ground!

## ON FOUR FEET
A zebra baby can walk as little as twenty minutes after it is born, and can run soon after. It learns to recognize its mother by her smell.

## LITTLE HORNS

Adult giraffes have two horns. Females have hairy tufts on theirs, while males have knobbly ends. A baby giraffe is born with its horns lying flat, but they grow and stand up straight after a few days.

## BIG BABY

Giraffes are the tallest animal on the planet. Fully grown, they reach between 14 to 19 ft (4 and 6 m) and their 6-ft (1.8-m) legs are taller than many people! The babies are about this height when they are born.

## BLACK AND WHITE

Is a zebra black with white stripes, or white with black stripes? Probably white, as its underside is white, with black stripes stretching up across its back and down its legs. Underneath the fur, though, a zebra's skin is black! Their pattern helps to keep them cool, and stops nasty biting insects from zooming in on them.

**DID YOU KNOW?**
Zebras sleep standing up, and members of the herd signal if a predator comes close.

# DEER AND ANTELOPES

These creatures have many things in common, but they belong to different animal families. Both have hoofs, and feed in similar ways. However, deer grow antlers but antelopes have horns.

## NYALA ANTELOPE

These African creatures grow up to have long, curved horns on the males. The babies are small, and stay hidden in long grass for two or three weeks.

## SIKA DEER

These little cuties grow fast, and by eight months old are as big as their mother. They can jump very high, and are excellent swimmers!

## GRANT'S GAZELLE

Gazelles are a member of the antelope family, and related to goats, sheep, and cows. Their babies are called fawns. They escape from predators by running quickly and springing high in the air with all four feet.

## ELK

Fully-grown, the elk is one of the largest kinds of deer. The babies are born in late spring, and have pale spots on their fur to help them stay hidden in shadowy places.

# DID YOU KNOW?

An antelope keeps its horns throughout its life, but deer lose their antlers and grow new ones every year.

## DANGEROUS TIMES

The first few weeks of a deer or antelope's life can be the most dangerous, as the babies are not strong or fast enough to escape from predators. Most mothers hide their babies in long grass, and keep checking on them and feeding them every few hours. Some have an extra, secret disguise: they have no smell, so predators cannot sense they are there if they remain unseen.

# WILD DOGS

Pet puppies are tiny, cute, and helpless – and so are their wild cousins! Dogs, foxes, jackals, coyotes, and wolves all have babies called cubs or pups. Many other animals have only one baby at a time, but dogs give birth to between three and 12 pups. One set of pups born together is called a litter.

## RED FOX
Tiny newborn foxes are called kits, and have brown fur rather than red. They are born with their eyes closed and cannot see until they are around two weeks old. They are deaf and toothless, too!

## DINGO
These wild dogs live mostly in Australia, and grow to a similar size to a golden retriever. They make a den for their pups in rocks, hollow logs, and abandoned burrows.

## COYOTE
Coyote mothers, like all mammals, feed their babies milk to begin with. As the pups grow bigger, the parents will regurgitate (throw up) chewed food for the little ones to eat.

## AFRICAN WILD DOG
Also called the African painted dog, because of its bold patterns, these animals have up to 20 pups in one litter. Their huge dark ears help them stay cool and hear over long distances.

## BAT-EARED FOX
Once these babies have grown too big to drink their mother's milk, the father takes over with childcare. He feeds, grooms, and looks after the pups.

## WOLF

Wolves roam great distances in groups, or packs, to allow them to hunt animals much larger than themselves. Their famous howl is used to send messages to other members of their pack, even if they are a long distance away. The pack leaders are a male and female which give birth to all the babies. The other wolves in the pack help to look after these babies.

# DID YOU KNOW?
On a clear night, across open ground, a wolf's howl can be heard up to 10 miles (16 km) away.

# MONKEYS AND APES

Primates – the group that includes monkeys and apes – come in all sizes, from the pygmy marmoset that could fit in the palm of your hand, to the giant gorilla, which can weigh twice as much as a baby elephant!

### GORILLA
A newborn gorilla weighs less than a human baby, but develops much faster. Although they are helpless to begin with, they can crawl when they are two months old, walk at about nine months, and look after themselves when they are three years old.

### CHIMPANZEE
Most chimps give birth to one baby at a time, and care for it for a long time. The baby clings to the fur on its mother's tummy until it is big enough to ride on her back.

### BONOBO
Closely related to the chimpanzee, the bonobo has pink lips and a black face, and is slimmer than a chimp. They are much less aggressive in their social group. A mother has a baby every five to six years, and looks after it for up to five years.

## CLEVER CREATURES

Like humans, monkeys and apes can hold tightly onto small objects using their fingers and thumbs. Very useful for finding food!

## PLAY TIME

Baby monkeys often have a completely different shade of fur from their parents. They spend their time eating, sleeping – and playing!

## MACAQUE MONKEY

A baby macaque has a pale face and pale fur, but as it grows its fur becomes darker and its face looks pinker. Its bottom is pink, too! They spend much of their time finding food in the trees, which they store in their cheek pouches.

# DID YOU KNOW?

These macaques are good at swimming, and go into the water when they are as young as two days old.

# SEALS AND PENGUINS

These animals have a tough life, living in some of the world's coldest places and swimming in icy oceans. They have thick skin, lots of fat (blubber), and the babies are covered in warm, fluffy fur or feathers.

## ELEPHANT SEAL

When fully grown, an elephant seal has a long, dangling snout that looks like an elephant's trunk. The babies are much cuter! They drink rich milk for a few weeks and then their mother leaves them and returns to the open ocean.

## ATLANTIC SEAL

These babies are born with soft white fur which is replaced as they reach a few weeks old. They breed on land but adults spend around two-thirds of their time at sea.

## GENTOO PENGUINS
It's easy to tell a gentoo penguin from other kinds, by its bright orange beak and long tail. The mother lays two eggs in a nest built on the ground.

## CHINSTRAP PENGUIN
The chicks of this species stay in their rocky nest until they are about a month old. They lose their baby fluff a month later, and are ready to swim out to sea.

## WALKING AND SWIMMING
Sea lion babies are born with their eyes open, and can swim almost immediately. An adult sea lion will twist its tail forward to help it walk on land, and even the babies can do this within an hour of being born.

# DID YOU KNOW?

Male emperor penguins do not eat for two months while they care for their eggs.

## EMPEROR PENGUINS

The largest of all penguins, these tough creatures spend winter on the Antarctic ice, braving the biting winds and temperatures below -40°F (-40°C). This is when they lay their eggs. The father stands guard over his egg, holding it off the cold ground on his feet and keeping it sheltered with a feathery pouch.

# MAMMAL BABIES

Mammals that live on land usually walk on four legs, and have furry coats, clawed feet, and very, very cute babies! They feed these babies with milk until they are old enough to eat solid food.

### RACCOON
Raccoons are excellent climbers, and the babies often spend their early life in a tree home called a den. After about 12 weeks the babies are big enough to climb down and search for food on their own.

### MEERKAT
Large groups of meerkats, called colonies, dig underground burrows and have their babies inside. The adults teach the youngsters how to hunt and stay safe.

## SKUNK
A mother skunk will have four to seven babies, called kits, in one litter. She is very protective and will spray a foul, stinky liquid from her rear end to keep enemies away.

## SEA OTTER
The sea otter spends most of its time in the water, and has a thick furry coat to keep it warm. The mother usually has just one pup which is so fluffy it floats!

## DID YOU KNOW?

When they are born, baby ring-tailed lemurs are about the size and weight of an ordinary chocolate bar!

### RING-TAILED LEMUR

Lemurs live only on the island of Madagascar, off the coast of Africa. Many of them spend much of their time in the treetops, but ring-tailed lemurs like to climb down and look for food on the forest floor. The baby holds on tight to the fur on its mother's chest for about two weeks, and then is strong enough to cling on to her back, and to reach out to grab branches.

# BABY BIRDS

Birds are totally different from mammals in the way they have babies. They lay eggs which protect the unborn chicks until they are strong enough to hatch out. Many parents bring food to the nest until their youngsters are big enough to fly or wander off alone.

## OWL
Owl chicks, or owlets, learn to climb before they can fly. They scuttle around the branches, and can use their wings, beak, and claws to help them climb.

## EMU
These giant birds lay giant eggs, which have a dark green shell. The chicks have soft, fluffy feathers and are striped for camouflage.

## CARIBBEAN FLAMINGO
The bright pink adults start life as small, dirty white chicks with a straight beak. Unlike most birds, the parents produce a milky liquid for their chicks to drink.

## WILD DUCK
A cute baby duck hatches from its egg with its eyes open, ready to look after itself. They stay in the nest for only a day or two.

## SWAN
Baby swans are called cygnets, and look very different from their long-necked, white-feathered parents. They hatch in nests on the ground, made of sticks and leaves.

## OSTRICH CHICKS
The ostrich is the largest bird in the world, and its wings stretch 6.5 feet (2 m) when opened out – more than the height of an average man. They cannot fly, but use these wings for steering when they run fast. They are also helpful as a sunshade for their babies! Newborn chicks can be as big as a hen, and grow to adult height within half a year.

# DID YOU KNOW?

An ostrich egg is 6 inches (15 cm) long and can weigh the same as 24 chicken eggs.

# MARSUPIALS

Marsupials are a special kind of mammal. They feed their babies on milk, but in a pouch that keeps them safe. The babies are tiny and bald as they are born much earlier than other mammals.

## KANGAROO
When born, a kangaroo is no bigger than a bee. It claws its way through its mother's fur to find a way into her pouch, where it drinks her milk.

## ROCK WALLABY
Like other marsupials, a baby rock wallaby's arms develop before its back legs and tail, to allow it to crawl into its pouch.

## WOMBAT
Wombats dig a lot to make their burrows in the ground. The opening of their pouch faces backward to prevent dirt from getting in as they fling earth back with their claws.

**KOALA**
A koala mother carries her baby in her pouch for about half a year. For another half year, it will hitch a ride on her back as she clambers through the branches to find food.

## KANGAROOS

The largest of all marsupials, kangaroos are the national symbol of Australia. Their back feet are so long that they cannot walk normally; they have to hop or crawl, and can't go backward! A mother can have more than one baby in her pouch, of different sizes. She even produces a different type of milk to feed the bigger one!

# DID YOU KNOW?

The baby of any marsupial animal is called a joey – it's not just the name for a baby kangaroo.

# HIPPOS AND RHINOS

## SUN SAFETY

Hippos are most active at night, when their delicate skin is safe from the sun. By day, they hide in the water, and produce a special red oil that acts as a sunblock.

## HEAVY HIPPO

A newborn hippo weighs around 100 pounds (45 kg), roughly the same as a skinny teenager. They can close their nostrils and ears to keep out water, and drink their mother's milk underwater!